LIZ LOCHHEAD

Liz Lochhead was born in Motherwell in 1947 and graduated from Glasgow School of Art in 1970 from the Department of Drawing and Painting. She had by that time, though, shifted her creative loyalties and preoccupations – and written most of the poems that came out in her best-selling (for poetry anyway!) first collection of poems *Memo for Spring* in 1972. It's just been re-published in a fiftieth-anniversary edition. She has since produced a further three collections and a *Selected Poems*, all still in print from Polygon, with the latest, *Fugitive Colours*, published in 2016.

The 1980s marked a transition from teaching art in secondary school to becoming a full-time writer and working on her first attempts at drama for the stage. Her first full professional production was *Blood and Ice* at the Traverse Theatre in Edinburgh in 1982. Since then her more than a score of stage plays have included *Mary Queen of Scots Got Her Head Chopped Off*, *Good Things*, *Perfect Days* and *Thon Man Molière*, based on the life of her favourite dramatist. All of these are published by Nick Hern Books, as are many of her stage adaptations, including *Dracula*, Molière's *Tartuffe*, *Miseryguts* (based on *Le Misanthrope*) and *Educating Agnes* (based on *L'École des Femmes*); as well as versions of *Medea* by Euripides (for which she won the Scottish Book of the Year Award in 2001), and *Thebans* (adapted mainly from Sophocles' Oedipus and Antigone).

Liz was the second Makar, or National Poet of Scotland, from 2011 till 2016, and received the Queen's Gold Medal for Poetry for 2015.

Liz Lochhead

MEDEA

after Euripides

NICK HERN BOOKS

London

www.nickhernbooks.co.uk

A Nick Hern Book

This version of *Medea* first published in Great Britain in 2000 as an original paperback by Nick Hern Books Limited, 49a Goldhawk Road, London W12 8QP

This edition first published 2022

Copyright in this version of *Medea* © 2000, 2022 Liz Lochhead

Liz Lochhead has asserted her rights to be the author of this work

Cover photography by Peter Dibdin

Typeset by Nick Hern Books
Printed in Great Britain by Mimeo Ltd, Huntingdon, Cambridgeshire PE29 6XX

A CIP catalogue record for this book is available from the British Library

ISBN 978 1 83904 115 0

Woodland
CARBON
www.woodlandcarbon.co.uk
NICK HERN BOOKS
Printed on Carbon Captured paper

This version of Liz Lochhead's *Medea* was first produced by
National Theatre of Scotland, and performed at The Hub,
Edinburgh, as part of the Edinburgh International Festival, on
10 August 2022. The cast and creative team was as follows:

JASON	Robert Jack
GLAUKE	Alana Jackson
NURSE	Anne Lacey
KREON	Stephen McCole
MEDEA	Adura Onashile
MANSERVANT	Adam Robertson
UNDERSTUDY	Pierce Reid
CHORUS	Lola Aluko
	Leyla Aycan
	Lindsey Campbell
	Janette Foggo
	Pauline Lockhart
	Fletcher Mathers
	Eileen Nicholas
	Wendy Seager
	Brooke Walker
	Bea Webster
SUPERNUMERARIES	Brian McKigen
	Euan Mitchell
	Douglas Yannaghas
CHILDREN	Frieda Bazie Gilmore
	Iggy Bazie Gilmore
	Otis Bazie Gilmore
	Kamsi Jibulu
	Amari Tadé
	Samuel Jude Walker
Director	Michael Boyd
Intimacy Coordinator	Vanessa Coffey
Casting Director	Laura Donnelly CDG
Lighting Designer	Colin Grenfell

Composer and Performing Musical Director	James Jones
Understudy Percussionist	David Kerr
Fight Director	Janet Lawson
BSL Consultant	Brooklyn Melvin
Assistant Director	Jaïrus Obayomi
Movement Director	Janice Parker
Set and Costume Designer	Tom Piper
Sound Designer	Josh Robins
Voice Director	Jean Sangster
Lighting Supervisor	Karin Anderson
Personal Assistant	Vaila Anderson
Deputy Stage Manager	Louise Charity
Sound Supervisor	Fraser Cherrington
Lighting Supervisor	Tom Davies
Company Manager	Michael Dennis
Production Manager	Chris Hay
Costume Assistant	Nicki Martin-Harper
Costume Technician	Lesley McNamara
Stage Manager	Jennifer McTaggart
Assistant Stage Manager	Susan McWhirter
Lighting Programmer	Tamykha Patterson
Costume Supervisor	Morag Pirrie
Assistant Stage Manager	Anna Reid
Producer	Lesley Anne Rose
Technical Swing	Ruben San Roman Gamez
Chaperones	Chloé Brown
	Cat Perry
	Claire Randall
	Gary Sloan
BSL Interpreters	Greg Colquhoun
	Yvonne Strain
Audio Describers	Bridget Stevens
	Lydia Kerr
Captioner	Ben Poots

Set built by the Citizens Theatre, Glasgow

Set painted by Jason Dailly, Lisa Greaf and Lisa Kellet

National Theatre of Scotland is a Theatre Without Walls. We don't have our own building. Instead, we bring theatre to you. From the biggest stages to the smallest community halls, we showcase Scottish culture at home and around the world. We have performed in airports and tower blocks, submarines and swimming pools, telling stories in ways you have never seen before. We want to bring the joy of theatre to everyone. Since we were founded in 2006, we have produced hundreds of shows and toured all over the world. We strive to amplify the voices that need to be heard, tell the stories that need to be told and take work to wherever audiences are to be found.

Artistic Director & Chief Executive	Jackie Wylie
Executive Director	Brenna Hobson
Chair	Seona Reid DBE

For the latest information on all our activities, visit us online at **www.nationaltheatrescotland.com** or follow us on:

Twitter	@NTSOnline
Facebook	NationalTheatreScotland
YouTube	ntsonline
Instagram	ntsonline

SUPPORT NATIONAL THEATRE OF SCOTLAND

Our wonderful donors and supporters help us to:

- Make amazing big shows and wee shows to take all over Scotland, from the grandest theatre stages to the tiniest village halls
- Share stories which reflect the diversity of Scotland – its people, places and history
- Nurture and support Scottish theatre artists
- Reach audiences near and far: on tour, on cinema screens, and across digital platforms
- Create world-class drama and education resources for every school in the country
- Represent Scotland on the international stage

How to support:

- Become a regular Individual Donor
- Corporate Sponsorship
- Introduce us to a Charitable Trust or Foundation
- Remember us in your will
- Attend one of our special fundraising events

Find out more:

Visit **www.nationaltheatrescotland.com/support**

Contact **development@nationaltheatrescotland.com**

An earlier version of *Medea* was commissioned by Theatre
Babel as part of the company's Greeks Project, and first
performed at The Old Fruitmarket, Glasgow, on 17 March 2000,
with the following cast:

MEDEA	Maureen Beattie
JASON	Stephen Hogan
KREON	Finlay Welsh
GLAUKE	Dawn Steele
NURSE	Carol Ann Crawford
MANSERVANT	John Kazek
GUARD	Gareth Williams
CHORUS	Amanda Crossley
	Alexa Kesselaar
	Barrie Hunter
	Raymond Short
	Rebecca Rodgers
	Vari Sylvester
	Ali de Souza
Director	Graham McLaren

It was subsequently performed at Assembly Rooms, Edinburgh,
as part of the Edinburgh Festival Fringe, in August 2000, with
the following cast changes:

GUARD	Paul Needham
CHORUS	Dierdre Davis
	Katy Hale
	Collette Murray

The production toured in 2000, with the following cast changes:

JASON	Bruce White
MANSERVANT	Michael Nardone
NURSE	Jo Cameron Brown

It returned to Assembly Rooms, as part of the Edinburgh Festival Fringe, in August 2001, with the following cast changes:

JASON	Duncan Duff
MANSERVANT	John Kazek
NURSE	Carol Ann Crawford
CHORUS	Pauline Knowles

Introduction
Liz Lochhead

When asked how I came to write my version of Euripides' *Medea* – unbelievably it's more than twenty years ago now – I have to be honest and admit it wasn't something I had been burning to do. No, it was a first-the-phonecall project, as have been quite a few of the adaptations for the theatre I have ended up working on over the years. In this case my friend Graham McLaren of Theatre Babel, a company whose whole *raison-d'être* was making new productions from the classic repertoire, was determined his current 'Greeks' project, exploring the most fundamental works in the evolution of drama, was exactly the right next thing for him to put his heart and soul into. And he was both adamant and persistent that I was the writer for a brand-new take on *Medea*.

I have never found working on the texts of great plays by writers as various as Molière (three times over the decades, making all three of his greatest plays in rhyming couplets, in three very different versions of 'Scots') – or riffing on Chekhov, or Schnitzler even, as I did quite recently – any less 'creative' than working on 'my own stuff'. It's *almost* as demanding and difficult to be an adapter, though in the end, when I have managed to get what felt (to me at least) like a handle on the task in hand, just as deeply satisfying.

You start with your gut instinct. Can I sense something, even if I don't yet know what, which other recent versions seem to me to be missing and which I'd like to try to bring out? In this case I had read a couple of excellent recent English translations of *Medea* and told Graham so. One of them would work very well for Theatre Babel, surely? I had no desire to repeat, badly, the good work of another writer. But he wouldn't let me off the hook. He was sure there was a new version of this play in me and insisted I could change things as I saw fit. (Exactly as the Greeks themselves did – just Google or check out your Robert

Graves and you'll see there are many, many conflicting stories surrounding the myth of Medea, though Euripides' version of her caps the lot for all time in its terror and pity.) I think it was this freedom Graham promised made me eventually agree to try to make this version, and my grateful thanks go to him.

This was in the very late 1990s. At the time, I was deep into the second draft of a play all of my own devising. A contemporary comedy set in the here-and-now, booming, suddenly trendy and confident post-City-of-Culture Glasgow and was about a successful, well-off, self-made woman who, single and just about to hit her fortieth birthday, was suddenly desperate to give birth to a child. Thus there was a frisson of slightly perverse attraction in the notion of my next play being – in every way – exactly the opposite: a tragedy, absolutely timeless and ancient, about a woman driven by female desperation of a quite different sort, to killing her children.

Which is not a very elevated reason for taking on a Great Classic Play, but it's the truth. My method? I started off by reading all the versions of *Medea* in translation I could find. And the footnotes in English in the Greek editions arguing the nuances of particular words he'd used. I was trying to understand – imperfectly, of course, but as exactly as I could – what was articulated in an argument, the implications of the imagery he used, and to somehow intuit what seemed to me to be its unique and thrilling tone.

From the word go I was thrilled by Euripides' astonishing and bold irony, his black, black humour. I was delighted to work on a text so outrageous, so impious. How jaggedly colloquial as, being faithful to it in my fashion, it was turning out to be. What fun I was having. Was it 'in Scots'? Now, I have no nostalgic, sentimental or political axe to grind about language or dialect, and I have learned that if one allows those writing the blurbs advertising a production to label it as being 'in Scots' even people who live here, even people who actually grew up here and (sometimes) speak it, can erroneously think they might not understand it. There is absolutely nothing in this play *in performance* that any English speaker won't. Three of the principal characters – the Nurse, the Manservant and the King – use a Scots-inflected English; Medea and Jason are outsiders so don't; the Chorus and the young 'other-woman' Glauke might have Scots *accents*, but that's about it. (Plays, as they come alive for me, come alive first of all as voices, as sounds.) Well, I was writing this for one particular one-off (we assumed) production from what was a Scottish theatre company after all, and I was relishing the harshness, the gutsiness and grit as my version was emerging. Euripides seemed to me very different from what the scholars called 'the sublime and mellifluous Aeschylus' and 'the grand and stately, morally complex, poetic Sophocles'.

If an English or American or Australian or whatever company wanted to use my version of this play – because it does differ from Euripides' – all they'd have to do is ask and we could work on it.

I am writing these notes the night before the readthrough for what will be only the second full professional production of this play. This time a co-production between the National Theatre of Scotland and the Edinburgh International Festival. (Something I thought would never happen till I was dead, if then: an actual posh EIF production of a play of mine. I'm a Fringe person, really.) The EIF, born 1947, is seventy-five years old this summer and I'll be seventy-five this Christmas, so, sentimentally and superstitiously, I hope there just might be something right and fitting about this? We had to pandemic-postpone in 2020 and again in 2021 – and now, in 2022, it's finally happening.

Back in the year 2000 and again in 2001, with the most hard-fought-for and skimpy shoestring funding, *Medea,* with my brilliant friend Maureen Beattie in the lead role – no wonder she got all these awards – was a big sell-out hit on the Edinburgh Festival Fringe. There were a few nights of a Scottish tour in other cities; we got to go to a Festival of Greek theatre in Cyprus and play in an amphitheatre; we were invited and went to the prestigious Toronto Theatre Festival; we did one afternoon reading in the National Theatre in London. Then the money ran out.

More than two decades on, a completely new Scottish (or based here in Scotland) company, many of whom I have worked with before, assembled and cast by my old friend Michael Boyd –

Sir Michael Boyd who ran the RSC for a decade – Michael who I have known since he was a nineteen-year-old student and already a wunderkind director and theatre-deviser – Michael who, when he was in his early twenties and a trainee director at the Belgrade Studio in Coventry, worked with late-starter me (I was thirty) on an admittedly complete failure of a show wherein he nevertheless taught me so much that it eventually became *Blood and Ice,* my first play. Michael and I knew we could never, would never, do this play unless we found the right Medea. How thrilled I was when he told me he had found this in Adura Onashile, who lives here in Glasgow, is stunningly beautiful, an award-winning actor, writer and film director herself. She is going to be fantastic. We start tomorrow.

Tonight though, I am toasting Euripides. I do remember more than two decades ago, as I began my version of *Medea*, reading, disagreeing profoundly sometimes, some of what was written about this man Euripides. How could that feminist critic find him misogynist? Had she been reading the same play as I? It seems to me astonishing and wonderful that the passionate diatribe against the palpable unfairness of woman's lot Euripides gives to his Medea was written and performed by a male to an all-male audience in Athens way back as this brand-new form of storytelling we now call 'drama'. More than 500 years BC. Something else I read speculated that – as Greek dramatists often performed their own plays – his predilection for female protagonists might well have been because he was a brilliant 'travesty actor' writing himself great roles. Now we were talking...

Eventually, sticking with a couple of pedantic and not-at-all speakable Victorian and even earlier translations, ones that would elucidate without influencing the language in any way, I simply used Euripides' *Medea* as a complete structural template. Then let go and did, at a crucial part of the drama, change *his* narrative and put what I felt was more pressure on Medea, raised the stakes to make it even more inevitable that she do what she does by inventing an encounter with the 'other woman' – Glauke, Princess of Corinth – who does not appear in the Euripides' version at all. In my not-very-pure account of this myth, this play, Medea is not supernatural, not an immortal, but is all too human. Even if she does have some spectacular poisons and skills, I chose not to interpret them as spells.

The mixed marriage between Jason and Medea in my version isn't between a man and demi-goddess, but between a man and a woman. I'd say this is why *Medea* will continue to mean as much as it always has to human beings – for as long as our species survives.

Glasgow, 2022

MEDEA

Liz Lochhead

after Euripides

Note

The people of this country – Corinth – all have Scots accents.
Their language varies from Scots to a Scots-flavoured English,
they are all individuals but their language does not vary in
respect of class or status.

A woman is talking to herself and us. This is the NURSE.

NURSE
I wish to all the Gods it had never sailed   the Argo
had never set its proud prow atween the humped blue rocks
of distant islands   forced itsel through straits
breisted waves to land on unlucky Kolchis   why?
why   did the sun ever heat up the soil
in which there split that seed
that sproutit from sapling to a tall tree of girth enough
to be felled to build its keel?   why was it ever oared?
why crewed wi heroes fit to filch the Golden Fleece?
adventurers!
my lady Medea would never then have sailed wi Jason
daft for him   doted!
had Jason   lethal Jason   never
landed thon fatefu Argo on her faur island hame
love-struck Medea would no
have helped him yoke the fiery oxen
tellt him   aye   to sow the dragon's teeth
but gied him the hert and the will and the wey
to ding doon deid every last yin o thon warrior army
that sprung up bristling oot the grunn agin him
she would no have   for his sake
swicked Pelias' dochters into killing their faither
killed her ain brither   they say
oh whit do they no say?
folk here aye say mair than their prayers

for Jason's sake she fled here to Corinth
wi Jason and their bairns   ingratiatin hersel
sookin in   a fawning exile   a foreigner
for his sake

now it all sours on her   see how he's turned
brave Jason's bedded a new bride   Glauke
dochter of Kreon the King   a princess of this land

and Medea left to rot
among the spilte and wastit love she's stuck wi
she's chucked out like
an old coat that nae langer fits him
nae wonder Medea winna be comforted   shivers
stinks of fear   canna eat
canna sleep   greets till she can greet nae mair
stares at the cauld grunn   greets again   greets sair
try soothing her   she's a stone
in kindness leave her be   she rolls in her rags
claws at hersel   keening
too late she screams remorse for a faither loast
a land abandoned   the betrayals
she made for Jason who faur faur worse betrays her noo
too late   too late she learns she should
have clung to what she had
the children   she looks on them with empty eyes
as if they're nothing to her
I'm feart for her   fear her
I shut my eyes and see Medea
creepan through the labyrinthine palace
follying her hatred like a thread
I dream of a dagger thrust in yon double bed
skewering the lovers thegither
I see the skailt blood of Kreon the King

she's capable of onything

A handsome young strong MANSERVANT *enters with the*
CHILDREN.

MANSERVANT
well auld yin   my lady's lady
what are you daen dithering here
girning on aboot the griefs of your betters?
they wouldnae greet for you

NURSE
here're these sweet wee children playing
no a care in aw the warld
what are grown up griefs to bairns?   play away
for your mither things could not be worse

MANSERVANT

oh could they no?
so much you know auld yin
that's no what I heard I tell you

NURSE

what did you hear?

MANSERVANT

I'm saying naething

NURSE

tell me what you heard

MANSERVANT

to say naething is already to have said too much

NURSE

speak to me   we're slaves
baith in the same sair place in this catastrophe

MANSERVANT

I know it and when I greet it will be for masel
I heard talk   they never saw me
it was where the old men play at draughts and blether
and mibbe blethers is aw it is   I hope so
word wis   King Kreon   and he's the boss
means to banish these bairns and their mither

NURSE

no Jason
he wouldna!   their mother mibbe
but no his best his maist beloved bairns

MANSERVANT

things cheynge   this new Jason the day
does not give a tuppenny fuck for anybody in this hoose

NURSE

misery piled on misery and mair of it
new agony afore the first has done its worst

MANSERVANT

wheesht   say naething
if things are this daurk

your mistress will ken aw aboot it
soon enough

NURSE

bairns do you hear what a faither you have?
I wish he were   no I'll not say it
I'll no wish my lord and master dead   but by Gods
the horror of how he treats those he should love!

MANSERVANT

get real old woman   what's the world about?
Jason can do so Jason does
hello bride bye bye bairns

NURSE

away in you go my bairnies   watch them man
keep them away from their mother   her hurt eyes of hate
what would she no do?
harm   all harm
to your enemies   Medea   no those you love!

The first primal cry from MEDEA *inside.*

there there wheesht my wee loves my bairnies
your poor mither   she's no right   run
keep away from her   thon's no your mother
the state she's in

The MANSERVANT *hurries them indoors.*

From off MEDEA *cries out in a voice that is not Scots but a foreigner speaking good English – an 'incomer voice'.*

MEDEA

Why don't you bloody die you
cursed litter of a cursed mother?
I hate my life and all I've done in it
I wish I'd never made you with your hated father
let it all crash around us   ah the ruins it's in!

NURSE

my marrow curdles to hear her curse what she most loves
is it no true the grand and horrid
passions of the high and mighty
rule them more cruelly

than they   the rulers   rule us humble folk?
a quiet life   we're   thank Gods   too dull
to draw doon the vengeance of the
ayeways angry Gods that look down and ayeways punish
them who think theirsels somebody

Another – the second – primal cry from MEDEA *inside.*

Enter CHORUS OF WOMEN.

CHORUS

that cry   we heard it
knew it in our bones   it curdled our blood too

MEDEA *cries from inside again – for the third time.*

CHORUS

we are sorry for your sorrow   sister
is that how they cry in Kolchis   Medea?

NURSE

this house is a ruin   ashes
a cold hearth and the fire put out in it
for ever
he's lording it lolling in bed with his royal bit
he's going to marry
she lies in cold ashes inconsolable

MEDEA *calls out from inside.*

MEDEA

I wish to all the Gods that I was dead and done with it

CHORUS

oh daft to wish for death
when it comes soon enough
without you tempt it
so your man fucks another?   fuck him
loves her?   tough   love him do you?
you'll grow out of that

we were not born yesterday
we are all survivors of the sex war
married women   widows   divorced
mistresses   wives   no virgins here

marriage over?   shame   that's the end of it
so get on with it

MEDEA

justice   Gods
look down on me and see my pain
I killed my own brother for you Jason
now I'll see you dead and that damned royal poppet too

CHORUS

bring her out and let us convince her
we're her friends   we can help her

NURSE

I'm in terror even to approach her
I know her
her cunning   her spells   her power
how far she'll go   and I'm feart o her
more even than I fear for her
she nurses her rage
like a lioness suckling her last living cub
claws at me   bull glares
would gore me   gash me
I'm anathema
that blank stare!

The NURSE *goes inside.*

There is silence from within. CHORUS *are listening, tense,
for something that doesn't come.*

CHORUS

that cry!

it was a cry we've heard
from the woman
opening the door to the telegraph boy in wartime

the cry from   the unquiet wife
opening the door
to the chequered hats of two policemen
late late on a foggy night

the cry from   the mother in the hospital corridor
when she sees the doctor's face

the cry from   the woman
whose lover's eyes have not quite lied
when she asked him
'tell me is there someone else?'

that cry
we have heard it
from our sisters   mothers   from ourselves
that cry
we did not know we knew how to cry out
could not help but cry
and we say

we are sorry for your sorrow   sister

is that how they cry in Kolchis   Medea?

rage yes rage at that traitor in your bed
salt and bitter are those tears
as the seas you sailed with him

> *Enter* MEDEA. *Not a girl but dignified, beautiful, calm and*
> *utterly reasonable. A foreigner, somehow exotic. She*
> *graciously approaches the chorus.*

MEDEA
women of all time   I'm here now
I know you've thought me strange   'standoffish'
     'a snob'
you've said of me   not understanding my shyness
my coolness merely masked my terror of being snubbed
no one loves a foreigner
everyone despises anyone the least bit different
'see how she ties her scarf'   'that hair   outlandish'
you walked by my house with eyes averted
turned your nose up at my household's cooking smells
'why can't she be a bit more like us?'
say you Greeks   who bitch about other Greeks
for not being Greeks from Corinth!
it's true I've not been   a woman's woman
I can say
I was never a woman at all until I met my man!
maiden Medea   my father's daughter   was a creature

who did not know she was born   she knew such
sweet freedom!
if it is a struggle in a bed or behind a bush engenders us
then it's when we fall in love that genders us
Jason   I am a woman now!

right out of the blue
humiliation   I was the last to know
the man who was more to me than my own life
is now the vilest man alive   my faithless husband

are we women not the most miserable
and mocked of all Gods' creatures?
our fathers scrimp and save
a dowry   a lavish wedding breakfast
to buy the man he sells us to
and then for better or worse   richer or poorer
in sickness or health   your sickness his health
this man lords it over us
our lives at the mercy of how his lordship feels
stuck with him and his every demand
the compensation?   they'll bear the arms!
oh yes   wartime
and they'll die for us!
well I'd three times sooner fight a war
than suffer childbirth once

if can find some way of paying Jason back
and the man who gives his daughter to him too
promise
will you women keep my secret?

we women are too weak   they say   for war
wrong us in bed though   oh man
we'll have your guts for garters

CHORUS
we promise you   we are women Medea
we know men   we know who's in the right
punish him for us Medea
but here's King Kreon   what will happen now?

Enter KREON *with the modest personal retinue of a very
powerful man.*

His voice is strongly Scots. Like the NURSE, *he is from this place. In common with all the other characters except* MEDEA, *he is blind and deaf to the chorus.*

KREON

you   glowering hate face
husband dumped you   has he?
so you hate him   the world's no wide enough
to haud you baith?   you'll be happy then
to hear my decree   I banish you
take your bairns and away you go
right now   far from our borders
I make the laws   and execute them
only when you're gone   will I sleep easy

MEDEA

I am in the worst of the storm and battered by it
I'm all alone   it's all over for me
no harbour   no haven
not a cave to shelter in
and this I ask you
what have I done to deserve this?

KREON

frankly I'm feart of you   why no?
feart you hurt my daughter   why no?
you're a clever quine and cunning
malice is your middle name
and your man threw you oot   who'd blame him?
I've heard you dared to threaten us
no just the groom-to-be but the bride and me the king
you'd do it too   Medea
I believe it   so it's in self-defence
nothing personal   I have to hunt you
raither that than clap you like a pussycat the now
then   too late   hear your tigress growl

MEDEA

I've heard this before
I'm oppressed by my reputation
the evil one   the witch   the clever woman
don't educate your daughters Kreon!

clever men are envied
and despised   the world has no use for them
fools think them foolish
the clever fear them
put them down   can't take the competition
but a clever woman
fie   it is to fly in the face of nature
an abomination
fear me?   I can't be very clever can I
or I'd not be in this pretty situation?

a man   a king
how could I   why should I
harm you who has   so far   done me no harm?
you're marrying your daughter to the man you chose
no harm in that
I can't fault you   but my man marrying your daughter?
it's him I hate
marry your daughter off and all the best
good luck to her she's done nothing to me
I hope they'll both be very happy

all I ask is a quiet corner
where I'll keep my head down I promise you
bring up my children like a poor and honest widow
saying nothing   saying nothing
you'll be my king   I your most humble maidservant
use me as you will   understand?
I'll do anything for you Kreon to show my gratitude

KREON
mild words but inside that seething cauldron   eh?
what's cooking?
I was not born yesterday Medea
the more you sweet-talk the less I trust
anybody who unleashes a tirade of hate
at least they're honest   you know where you are
but smiles   what's behind them?
get out   shut up
enough   get out   my mind's made up

MEDEA

I beg you by your daughter's life

KREON

dinna waste your words

MEDEA

have you no pity?

KREON

nane   just duty

MEDEA

oh Kolchis my home I cry for you

KREON

get back there then why don't you?

MEDEA

Kolchis   father

KREON

brother?
foul the nest there did you?   aye
I'd do the same to mine
if I did not drive you out   you murdering whore
like vermin from my doors

I love my bairn and next to her I love this place

MEDEA

love   I'd not wish love on anybody
not even on you my enemy

KREON

you are a pain to me

MEDEA

I am one pain from top to toe   I'm dying

KREON *snaps his fingers and his men bristle, stand to attention.*

KREON

men!   your escort awaits you madam
up you get

MEDEA

I'm on my knees

KREON

begging for bother and by Gods you'll get it

MEDEA

I'm going   I want to go   one favour though

KREON

in the name of all the Gods what is it and then will you go?

MEDEA

one day   one day of peace and preparation
my children to take final leave of their father
they don't hate him
and I to make some desperate provision
where   how
to save my two sweet sons   my daughter
you are a father too   have pity on them
you are a man   you should protect the helpless
the weak   the women   children
you are a Greek   a man of reason
civilisation   shall it be said
barbarians treat women and children better?
you are a king   you have the power to show mercy

KREON

I'm no a barbarian   I'm no a tyrant either
but by showing saftness
I've sometimes been the one to suffer for it in the past
so promise me Medea I'll no live to regret this
ach   you can have your day!

I say this though   and it's final
if the dawn comes up the morrow
and finds you or your brats still here within our borders
you're dead the lot of you
understood?

As KREON *exits with his retinue he talks aloud to himself.*

KREON

one day   that's no long enough
for any of the dirty tricks I'm feart o

CHORUS

one day!   one useless day!
poor woman we feel for you
where can you turn
who'll take you in
contaminated as you are
with the worst luck that Gods could chuck at anyone
it's an overwhelming sea   you're in it up to here

MEDEA

evil is deep indeed
but I'm not drowning
while dire times are about to overtake the happy pair
and all their crawling kith and kin

unless it furthered my plans
do you think I'd have crawled to him   fawning?
that man
I sucked up   begged   touched him
Gods but my flesh did creep
I'd rather have touched pitch or shit   I gagged but
swallowed it
the fool   he's a dead man   could have thwarted me
but granted me my glory day
to make three cold corpses
of him the king   of the bride-to-be
and of the man I hate

my darlings   my familiars
so many ways of killing and which shall I choose?
I could set a fire beneath the honeymoon suite
and roast them like herrings
or slip silently through the palace to where that bridal bed is made
and they'll have to lie on
with spilt guts where my sure dagger will spike them through

no   the female way is the best way
poison
the murderess's way and am not I the queen of it?
pretty poison   my certain expertise
never let it be said
the man was ever born who could do me down

Hecate   goddess of the deepest night
help me now
and the bitterest wedding breakfast I'll cook up for them
women   useless are we?
good for nothing?
good for evil
and evil all the good I ever want to be good for again!

CHORUS

water flows uphill   each stream's sucked up
backwards to its source
everything's upside down skew-whiff   insane
the way that men   we say the male sex only
can break their every sacred vow   and not fear
what nature'd do if she was a fraction as faithless
to physics' laws   we'd say we'd see the world implode

if women were once worms we've turned
we won't be put down the way that once we were
sling your old slanders of so called
female faithlesssness   sing us
something new

Medea   you set sail from your father's place
mad for a man you didn't know   braved
voyage   rocks   storms   straits   sailors' eyes
us strangers
only to be dumped   dishonoured in a foreign land

Enter JASON. *He goes firmly, directly, to* MEDEA.

his word is broken   all promises trashed
honour evaporated   another woman queens it in your
double bed

JASON *is a Greek too – but not from this place.*

JASON

it is not what you think!
it's not the first time   you waste yourself
I've seen it often
the way you will let your tongue run away with you
when a low profile   meek words
acceptance of the status quo

would have been the way to keep your home
your words don't worry me Medea   sticks and stones
they're straw and chaff   the worst of your curses
call me every vile thing that creeps I don't care
but Kreon is the King   you rant at him
are you crazy?   count yourself lucky
exile's all the punishment so far proposed

I feel bad about it
although you've brought it on yourself Medea
and I won't stand by and see you starve
or the children go short or want for anything
call me every low thing that crawls   I'll still care for you

you make it hard for me   I've always done my best
to calm him down   persuade him you should stay
I could have crept back to you in secret   would have
but you can't keep it zipped   you will talk treason
court your own banishment

MEDEA

I can't keep it zipped!

CHORUS

ha!

MEDEA

who   what   could be worse than you?
I'd call you coward   you piece of vomit   man
who is no man at all except you're man enough to come here
amazing   shamelessness never fails to amaze
d'you think it brave?   how dare you
shit on those you say you love and then come visiting?
where in the depths of your vile maleness do you get the nerve?
thanks for coming though
for I can ease my heart and watch you squirm
first things first

Out comes the LITTLE GIRL *running to her father crying out.*

LITTLE GIRL

daddy daddy daddy daddy daddy daddy

*JASON catches her up in his arms nuzzling into her face and
swings her round sobbing and laughing at the same time.*

JASON

my baby girl my darling darling

Behind them at the door terrified to enter, though she does, after her charge, comes hurrying the NURSE. *She hangs her head, flinching.* JASON *aproaches her, his* GIRL *in his arms.*

Behind them come the two BOYS *but before they can cross the threshold they are caught and restrained in the doorway by the* MANSERVANT, *also terrified, frozen.*

JASON *hands the* LITTLE GIRL, *struggling, into the* NURSE*'s arms.*

MEDEA

in the name of all the Gods take them inside
and keep them safe

JASON

boys!

They enter a few paces, stop.

be brave men   protect your little sister
it is your duty   go!

The MANSERVANT *snatches both of them and drags them inside.* JASON *paces across in front of the empty shut door and back. Arms flailing he silently mimes beating upon it knowing he can never enter through that door again nor ever again call that place home. He lets out a deep groan of anguish. Then calmly –*

first things first   Medea we must keep our children safe

MEDEA

first things first   I saved your life
and everybody knows it   each Greek that sailed with you
the whole caboodle who crewed the valiant Argo
knows it   without my magic
you could not have yoked the fiery bulls
in the field of death   nor sown the dragons' teeth
except I killed the serpent whose loathsome coils
looped the Golden Fleece
and who was its guardian who never slept

I killed it   I made you Jason!
betrayed my own father   my royal line
ran mad for you   after you   to Iolcus
more passion then than sense
I killed King Pelias to keep you secure
killed him by tricking his loving daughters to unwitting patricide
horror and another royal house destroyed

so I did then   now so do you
cheat on me   forsake me   bed a new bride

I gave you progeny
I'd have seen the force of a fresh liaison
were I barren but I bore you heirs   you swore by Gods
who must be dead so simply you broke all faith with them
my hand that held yours   I should cut it off
my knees that parted to let you easy come between
defile me   I'm fouled by even memory of your foul touch

so Jason you love me and wish me well?   pray tell
friend   sweet husband   where am I to go?
to my father's house perhaps?   oh yes
the father I betrayed to go with you
to Pelias' daughters?   they'd welcome me with open arms
that glad we did the old man in
this is the state I'm in   my friends and family are history
they hate me now
I made enemies of everyone I ever loved
for you   hurt those I had no need to hurt
for you   and in return
you make me the happiest woman in Greece
envied by all   'what a husband   lucky woman
   you could
one hundred percent trust him   to betray you!'
and here's his wedding present to himself
rootless penury for his discarded beggar wife and brats
oh Gods   there are proofs to tell
true gold from fool's dross
why no hallmarks stamped on the hearts of men?

CHORUS
a special anger   incurable
when lovely love is turned to hatred horrible

JASON

It seems that captain Jason must steer carefully
weather the tempest of your tirade
first   let's not exaggerate your role in my story
what you did for me Medea   you did it
in the first flush of lust for me let's face it
Aphrodite ought to get the credit
I was her darling   you were her mere instrument
a cunning woman   passion's puppet
wild to save my hide   well fine
I don't want to do you down   you brought it up though
inflated it out of all proportion
excuse me   I'd say you got more than gave quite frankly
dragged from the backwoods to civilisation
from brutish pigswill chaos to sweet law and reason
to this place where   Gods help them   they've made
    much of you
your cunning   your so sexy skills
if you were stuck in the sticks would they be sung about?
fame matters   oh it does   to you and me Medea
embrace it
it's our fate to be sung about not sing!

so much for all that
my marriage with the princess   it's not what you think
politics not passion   what I feel for her is nothing
to the sweet hot love I felt for you!

calm down   it's a good thing potentially   listen
we're on the run   blown in from Iolcos
all of us in every kind of deep shit till I land lucky
on the safe shores of marriage with the daughter of the main man
we're laughing!
what's eating you's the sex thing   it's not
that I've gone off you and fancy fresh young flesh to fuck
that's crude   I'd not have thought you'd have gone
for such mean and cliched thoughts Medea
I thought we knew each other better than that
and I don't want more kids   our brood
aren't they enough for both of us?   but
I'll not be nothing   nor will our boys be beggars

if they have new royal brothers in one united first family
it's for the best   don't you get it?

cunts for brains!   that's women   they're all the same
happy in the sack and all the world's a bed of clover
if that goes sour they go spare
and hate you   sex!
I wish there was another way to get us sons
without women the world would be a lovely place

CHORUS
well said Jason   your arguments are clever
we understand you do your wife a favour
by dumping her?   we beg to differ

MEDEA
maybe there's something wrong with me
I'm not like other people
I don't call them clever words that
would cloak evil in a plausible coat   wrap up this crap
in fancy phrases but one thing gives the lie to it

you did it behind my back

JASON
and if I'd told you?
listen to the unreasonable rage of you!

MEDEA
what it is is this   a statesman with a foreign wife
a savage   I'm an embarrassment to you

JASON
it's not what you think!
it's not for sex   it's not for snobbery
will you take a telling?   my royal wedding
it's for the future   it's for the children
to best protect them

MEDEA
protection?   poisoned prosperity?
I want no part of it

JASON
you'll see   eventually   you'll change your tune

MEDEA

you're wrong   but   torture and torment me

you're safe   I'm exiled abandoned and alone

JASON

you brought that on yourself

MEDEA

so I did!   I took another and abandoned you

JASON

you cursed the royal family

MEDEA

and yours Jason

JASON

we are going round in circles   this gets us nowhere
if you love our children leave them here Medea
you've fucked it up for you
your own big mouth got you exiled
still I'll do everything to help I can
cash   letters   I'll bust a gut to find
someone kind enough to take you in

MEDEA

screw your favours Jason   your foul friends
are no friends of mine

JASON

Gods are you watching?
I've done everything I could   for you   the kids
but you fling it all back in my face
you're a madwoman   it'll be the worse for you

MEDEA

go on   you're hot for her   go mount the cow
no malingering   get married man
your honeymoon will end in bitter tears

   Exit JASON.

CHORUS

desire   excess
and what desire is not excessive?

gets us into such trouble   does us in
drives us wild   makes us gluttons for punishment
oh Gods save us from that hotshot Cupid
and his brutal bullseyes

desire   excess
yes   better avoid it like the plague
or we've not the sense we were born with
no tangles in snarled sheets
no white nights in beds we should *not* be lying in
the best hope for us?
celibacy
or the next best thing   the cosy old
comfy married bed that's full of snores not battles

Gods save us from your miserable fate!
those of us who have been there before
are glad we are not there now

Gods send a miserable fate
to the one who locks away his heart
against the one he ought to love!

the things he said to you!
punish Jason for all of us Medea!

MEDEA

maybe Jason is not worth it
this pain   this pain
it paralyses me
you women are filled with ire on my behalf   I feel

emptied

perhaps Jason is right   my children would be better off
if I leave them here with their father
who loves them   he loves them
loves them and can offer them

everything

so much   so much
I love my children
can I leave them?

can I convince myself
to play the part of one of you until I learn it?
can I get philosophy?   sigh and say
'it happens'   'I am not the first and I won't be the last'
'in one hundred years it will be all the same'?
can I wear the mask of moderation?
can I?
as if when Cupid   Aphrodite's child
sweet Eros   drove the shaft of his arrow into my heart
as deep as the feathers   he
never
struck me   with love for Jason I'm stuck with for ever?

Enter GLAUKE – *a very pretty very young girl. Alone.*

CHORUS
we are amazed   how dare she?
here's the princess   proud Glauke
do you know this place?
this person you dare to approach?   we're quaking!
you are no feart   our Glauke
but maybe you do not entirely grasp the situation?

GLAUKE
Medea   my lady
I think it's daft we should fight like this
over a man   I am Glauke

MEDEA
I've heard of you   well   my girlie Glauke
what should we fight about instead?

GLAUKE
they say you are a witch   but I don't believe it

MEDEA
believe it   you bit of thistledown
one breath and I could blow
an allergen   an irritant   like you away

GLAUKE
I don't think so   I'm no some lightweight
bit of fluff   he loves me   I did not plan it

I never wanted my happiness should hurt another woman
do you know how much it hurts me
my happiness should hurt another woman?
but if a man no longer loved me   wanted freedom
he could have it
I'd be too proud to try and keep him
I don't hate you

MEDEA
do you expect me to say the same?

GLAUKE
that would not be reasonable
I can understand it if
at this moment   you think you hate me
Medea
I know what you and Jason have been to each other
in the past   these things are not easy
even though for you and Jason
everything has long been over
in the   man and wife sense of things
still you are your children's mother and father

MEDEA
thank you for these homilies

GLAUKE
you're welcome

MEDEA
it is always   useful
to view one's situation from the outside
see it from the point of view of the
other players in the drama

GLAUKE
I think so   otherwise we are
at the mercy of our passions

MEDEA
and Gods save us from such a fate!
the horror of being a prisoner
inside our own vile consciousness

unable to feel any pain but our own pain
torn internally by the snarling warring
imperatives of our passions
when a little empathy   imagination
walking the odd mile in the other person's shoes
would put everything into perspective

GLAUKE

I think you mock me
I may not be as clever as you
but I'm not stupid

MEDEA

you mock me
you may not be as clever as I
but I no longer have my husband

I made that man

GLAUKE

the past   the past
what's done is over!
you live inside your own self only
you live in the past

CHORUS

maybe someday if she lives so long she will suffer
but the girl Glauke is in love and happy now

MEDEA

I made that man
and now a fool of a slip of a girl
is to feast on what is left of him?

so 'everything has long been over
between Jason and me
in the   man and wife sense of things'?
you believed that?
the oldest lie in the book
we fuck all the time

GLAUKE

your womb is a dried up pod
rattling with shrivelled old seeds

you cannot give him any more babies
and my sweet firstborn
already is kicking in mine

MEDEA
indeed I tell you
take it as a friendly warning
in the   man and wife sense of things
between Jason and me
things have not yet begun

GLAUKE
I did not come here to quarrel
I am a civilised person   a Greek
these things happen   we   must
for the sake of the children if for no one else
make the best of things

I am to marry a man who is a father already
and who loves his children
I want him to be happy
Jason's wish for the children's future is
that they should stay with us
I'll be good to them   you may trust me
for Jason's sake

CHORUS
maybe someday if she lives so long she will suffer
but the girl Glauke is in love and happy now!

GLAUKE
think about this   calmly   when I'm gone
Jason would love to see his children
at our wedding
if you ever loved him   you will send them

> GLAUKE *exits on swift light feet.* MEDEA *paces silently.*
> *Seething.*

CHORUS
we think you show forbearance indeed Medea
the best that can be said in mitigation of the young
is that they are not yet old
her unkindness to you is unforgiveable

but maybe understandable?
we disliked her too
young beautiful women
in the wrong but righteous about it   are very hard to take

nevertheless she sounded sincere
about loving the children   even if it is for Jason's sake?
we were shocked at first   the mothers among us
when you said you'd leave them here with Jason
then we had to see it made good sense
you said yourself   so much   so much
you love your children
you must leave them?

MEDEA
hell will certainly have frozen over first!
her own words
have sealed her fate for ever
her father's doom and her husband's too
want my children at her wedding does she?
she shall have them
here's my hellish plan   I'm proud of it
listen   ladies   it is lovely!
I'll send the granny or the grunt
to get Jason again   I'll beg   grovel a bit
soft words   remorse I could have doubted him
the dad he is   he is the best dad
the new bride *so* sweet   I'm reconciled
I'll let the children stay

as if I could ever leave them
here   ringed around by my enemies
and taught to hate me!   never!
but they're my booby trap   oh my beauties
we'll do her in!
they'll take her my wedding gifts
a silken robe   a golden crown
that will brand her skull like redhot iron
and soon as the pretty flimsies touch her flesh she dies
the abortion in her womb
aborted like all her tomorrows   extinguished utterly
I'll snuff her out

and all who touch her will die as well
so toxic will be her corpse   oh yes

then   I can't say it   do it then
I'll kill the children   must
to save them
shall I let my sweet boys become cruel men like their father?
shall I let my daughter grow up to womanhood
and this world's mercy?   never!
I'll kill you first   my darlings
then when I've done for Jason utterly   I'll die happy

CHORUS
Medea   don't do it!   life   death   Gods's law
you cannot!

MEDEA
you could not   I must
how else will hard hearted Jason
learn his crying lesson?

CHORUS
tears for yourself   the bitterest taste you'll swallow

MEDEA
let's get a move on   ladies
less talk   more action
nurse!

NURSE *enters*.

nurse   send the man to run for Jason

NURSE *bobs a curtsey of obedience and goes back inside*.

CHORUS
you are not our kind
Medea   stop this!
what greater power than the love of a mother for her children?
every animal would die for its young
is that not nature's way Medea?
the mother sheep offers her own white throat
to the wolf and saves her lambs
cornered   the savage she-wolf
sacrifices herself for her helpless cubs

even the mild bird surprised in the nest
can be a winged and whirling devil
with a slashing beak

The MANSERVANT *enters from the house, bows to* MEDEA
and hurries off for JASON *as ordered. Even more urgently –*

a mother should die for her young   Medea
not be her children's murderess

hell itself will reject you
there is no reparation
you can never be purified of this crime   for humankind
it is our horror of horrors   how can you?
your sons you suckled at your breast
looked in their eyes and smiled on them
now you'd look them in the eyes
and slash them to their knees?
your daughter whose hair you brush and plait
who kisses your face and makes you laugh
when she lisps the
wrong words of the Kolchis song you taught her
oh will you wrap her own bright braid
around her throat and break her neck?

with the hardest of hearts

with the hardest of hands

still you cannot do this

Enter JASON. *He keeps his distance from* MEDEA.

JASON

here I am
for all your hatred I'm still here

what new malison?
Or have you   is it too much to hope for?
come to your senses

MEDEA

Jason I swallow my pride here
and   you know me   I don't find that easy
I beg you to forgive me   my foul temper

hurts me as much as it hurts you   believe me
but turn the other cheek   can't you?
for the sake of the sweet love we had in the past?
it's over   I know that now
I'm reconciled to it
I've been a fool   why rant and rave
at what cannot be helped?
you did not simply fall in love with a younger woman
I know that now   the politics!
it was beyond me at first I don't mind admitting it
too emotional to be rational like you always said
forgive me!   but of course I see now
it's for the best
the future of our sons and daughter is what matters now
and that's always been your first thought
forgive me   they must have royal brothers
I see that's why you're marrying

I wish you well   my old darling

we women have such petty natures sometimes!
good you're big enough to rise above
the dog eat dog   snarl for snarl
vicious circle I indulged in earlier

all I want to say is   I was wrong

The NURSE *comes out of the house with the* CHILDREN.

children!   don't shrink from us
we both love you
come kiss your daddy see like I do

MEDEA *kisses* JASON.

JASON *and the* CHILDREN *embrace.*

Gods the hell of it   the horror of knowing what I know
hiding what I must hide
the dagger agony to see them hug him
when never in this world
will they stretch out their sweet warm arms to me again
as long as they live   as long as any of us shall live
my heart breaks   I can't   I must

look dear hearts my quarrel with your dad is done
grown up anger!
your innocent eyes will not see
such a shameful scene again
my cheeks are wet with happy tears

CHORUS

we're crying too   we wish to all the Gods
there was not worse   we fear there's worse
to come

JASON

there's my old own sweet girl I recognise
it was a shock   I'm sure   and only natural
for a passionate woman to get a bit upset
it took a wee while   but now you
understand   that's excellent

boys! and daddy's own wee princess   are you listening?
your father's been giving it a lot of thought
your future

> JASON *takes his older* SON *and rumples his hair smiling at
> the other two, including them.*

JASON

one day   with your brother and sister
you'll be one of the top folk in Corinth
one of the ruling class   the highest in the land
    a leader
why not?   no hopes are too high
nothing's too good for Jason's children
and all you have to do to make your daddy happy
is grow up good and strong
eat   work   and play
play the game   play hard   play fair
fear nothing   your daddy   and the Gods   will
always be there for you   to protect you

now Medea   what's the matter?
more tears!   why?   nothing
in these words that should upset you

MEDEA
nothing   I was thinking of our children

JASON
well   be assured I'll take good care of them

MEDEA
I know you will   my tears are
just   a mother's
they need their father's hand   that's true
but I'm their mother
and when you wished them grown and powerful
it hurt that's all   for I won't see it
banished as I'll be   I'm not arguing
I understand
in my absence Glauke will accept them
my lovely children   who'd not love them?
ask   your bride
to ask her father to let the children stay

JASON
she's a gentle girl   is Glauke
I know they'll learn to love her

MEDEA
and she them!   I will help them   gifts!
fetch them nurse

The NURSE *hesitates. Then –*

NURSE
madam

NURSE *exits.*

MEDEA
no wedding without presents
I've a pretty pair to send her
in the children's name   a shawl
of the finest silk   a golden crown

NURSE *re-enters with gifts walking carefully.*

A box, and on top of it, a crown on a cushion.

MEDEA
boys take this box   and carefully
keep it closed   what is inside it must not crush
you hear me!   and darling girl
her bridesmaid   this crown
on its splendid cushion   but   hear me   do not touch!
do not touch
or you will dull its lovely shine

MEDEA *turns to* JASON.

my darling girl   to your new darling girl

JASON *bows and begins to exit,* MEDEA *continues to
herself as the* CHILDREN, *heads held high, begin to exit
slowly after their father with the presents proud and
pleased.*

to your lucky one with
the best man in all the world to bed her   Glauke
we'll decorate and crown her
wrap her for you like a present
Glauke in cloth of gold and with a golden crown

JASON *stops and turns.*

JASON
stop children!   this is too much Medea
we can't accept   I won't take them
Glauke has everything she needs   it would be greedy
she's not short of frocks
the palace groans under the weight of gold and silks already
save these for yourself

MEDEA
even Gods and millionaires like gifts
gold brings luck and I want your bride to have it
I know they'll learn to love her
she will love them too

JASON
that's true   let's take these lovely presents   children!
it would indeed be a shame to disappoint them

for they'll enjoy I'm sure
some small role in our ceremony

MEDEA

darlings deliver these petty tokens
then come back and tell your mama
that what she hoped would happen
happened   and Glauke smiled on you

Exit the CHILDREN *in solemn procession with* JASON.

CHORUS

that's it!
no hope for these bairns now
the road they walk on is to their death
not long!

MEDEA

she'll grasp the gold tiara   tara!
her own hands will crown her golden head
with her own bright death

it shines!
that robe of cloth of gold
and from its gleaming folds there rises   perfume
   amber
put it on!
she will   she'll shawl herself for a wedding
with her only marriage partner   death

CHORUS

miserable Jason
your bride   you did for her
you did for your own bairns too

we weep for you too Medea
mother of bairns
muderer of bairns
mother   murderer
what an end to a domestic commonplace!
the adulterous husband in the other woman's bed

The CHILDREN *and the* MANSERVANT *come back on.*
NURSE *pushes them inside, stays listening.*

MEDEA

nurse! away
go inside and get food ready for the children

> *The* NURSE *exits indoors.* MEDEA *moves closer to the*
> MANSERVANT

MANSERVANT

madam the bairns are reprieved
they're safe   no banishment
I waited at the palace   watched
when my lord Jason and the bairns came back
we were over the moon
word wis among us slaves   the quarrel's over
he was smiling   the   bride   thon Glauke
oor mistress in place of you   she
smiled too   picked up your wee lass
and sat her on her lap
hauding the bairn's wee hand against her belly
whisperin that she'd feel her baby brother kick
kissed her
then set her down again

MEDEA

tell me from the beginning

MANSERVANT

first thing
the children went up to her   saluted   curtseyed
the princess bowed and solemnly she
took your bonny presents
from your three bairns hands
madam   why turn away?
you're pleased are you no
to ken the bairns are spared?

> MEDEA *lets out a cry.*

what's wrang?

> MEDEA *lets out another even louder cry. Falls to her knees.*

did I speak out o turn?
I shouldna have tellt you about Glauke and your lassie

mind I never said your lassie liked it!
but it's good news shairly?

MEDEA
you said what you saw   my sweet and faithful servant
you   are not to blame

MANSERVANT
don't greet   my lady
I hate to see a bonny woman greet
others   madam   afore you
have been pairted from their bairns
what we canna cheynge we hae to thole

MEDEA
'thole it' I shall!
sweet servant I'll obey you
are you my faithful servant?

MANSERVANT
my lady Medea knows I am

MEDEA
and a man to trust?

MANSERVANT
tomorrow I go   with you into exile
you will find me   faithful   discreet   any service
I can render you
would be the pleasure   madam
no jist the duty   of a servant of a lady
as gentle and as beautiful as you
Medea   my good and lovely lady

MEDEA
there is   a certain small thing
no I cannot ask you

MANSERVANT
ask   anything

MEDEA
go back to the palace   no   it's no job for a man!
the wedding   can you come back and tell me
what the bride was wearing?

MANSERVANT
madam I'm no much of a man for describing frocks

MEDEA
I would be very grateful   in your debt indeed
truly I am sure you'll do it very well

MANSERVANT *bows and goes.*

The CHILDREN *enter, playing.* MEDEA, *alone with them,
looks upon her* CHILDREN.

children come and kiss your mama
you'll never know how much your mother loves you
children I am to say goodbye to you
the only things I have left to love in this life
I thought my heart was dead   but I still love you
goodbye before I see you grown
before I dress you for your weddings
or make your marriage beds

I choose this way but by the Gods it's sore
was it for this I suckled you and weaned you
laboured long to give you life
and the hopes I had
that you'd take care of me when I was old
and when I died would close my eyes
and clothe me for my coffin and a decent burial
the natural cycle of things   sweet thought
no hope   my beauties

I can't do it   I've lost my nerve
it's not right   their shining faces
it won't happen!
I'll take them now and run

what is wrong with me?   my enemies
off scot free and laughing at me?
come on   woman   do it   dare
are you so weak that motherlove can turn you?

shall I let my darlings
be toyed with by fate

fall into the savage hands of my enemies
run and they'll catch us   inevitible
inevitible I   save them first
the bride is crowned now   dressed
for her wedding and her bridegroom death
she's on her way   I know it
I'm on my way too   it's a cruel road
and crueller still the road I send my darlings on

my lovely boys   look at you
straight limbs   growing up strong
like your mother wants you to
give me your hands   your sweet lips!
such eyes!   be happy wherever you go

a hug   let mama hold you
the soft skin   sweet breath of children!
go inside   go inside
your mama's coming soon
to put you to your beds

> *The smaller* BOY *and the* LITTLE GIRL *go inside. The*
> *bigger* BOY *hesitates as if anxious to comfort his mother,*
> *offer to be a big boy. She smiles on him, touches his head to*
> *ressure him and he goes inside.*

what I am going to do   it is the worst
I know it   I must do it   I will do it

CHORUS
happy the woman who has no children
happy   that woman
she cannot then bear the pain of losing them
suppose you've raised them
they've survived   they thrive
they're up and perfect and you're proud of them
still the Gods can snatch them
death   disease   or war
can decimate our hopes
deaths of our children
this is the one pain the Gods should not ask us to survive

MEDEA

friends it's time   waiting's over
here he comes   quite out of breath
my good and faithful servant

MANSERVANT *comes running back on in terror, gasping.*

MANSERVANT

run   run   you bitch of hell
you really did it and you've done for us as well
a ship   a chariot   go

The NURSE *enters. Waits, afraid, stock still by the door, watching.*

MEDEA

what happened?

MANSERVANT

they're dead   as well you know
the princess   and Kreon the King her faither tae
deid   your poisons   bitch

MEDEA

I never heard you speak a finer word
as the royal correspondent
you're the man for me

MANSERVANT

you're mad   you really did it
by the Gods   you are gled you did it!

He staggers away from her in horror. But it is as if he is hypnotised.

MEDEA

calm down   catch your breath   my man
don't rush it   I want the whole story
sing up   spit it out
was it really such a horrible agonising way to go?
don't spare me one of the delightful details
the worse it was the better

MANSERVANT

the ceremony was done
Kreon kissed his daughter

shook the hand of her new husband
and took his leave
mindan the company how   in the great hall
there wad be feasting later
in the meantime there was dancing
whistling and cheering   applause from us servants
when the happy couple took the floor thegether

then did the bride's eye no alight
on the crown your lassie'd brocht her
nothing for it but she left her husband's side
laughing   ran and took it up
set it   gold on gold   on tap of her hair
when she pulled oot that soft silk shawl
there was a sigh went up at its shimmer
and she slipped into it
smoothing it over her breists and shooders
Jason whistled   she shimmied to the mirror
and stopped   stilled by her own
silvered beauty in the glass
stared smiling   totally taen on wi hersel
as why should she no be?

then   something hellish   before our eyes
her face cheynged colour   she swayed   reeled
across the floor   her legs buckling under her
only just made it to a chair
one of her servin lassies thought she was
only carrying on   that it was a joke
she whooped   then she saw
that her majesty was foaming at the mouth and
her eyes had turned all milky and opaque flickering
wi the pupils rolled back   and oh the colour she was
which was the colour of clay   of death
but she was gasping
ripping scarves of breath from the air
drawing them into her lungs
drowning   the servin lass cheynged her tune then
the shriek she let out   Gods   it made
all our blood run cold
stuck there as we were like stookies

wi the horror of it then it was all running feet
everywhere and the palace rang with shouts as they
tore the place apart looking for her faither

Jason just stood there the look on his face
one I hope never to see on another human face again

for the length of time it takes a good runner
to lap the racetrack she was slumped unconscious
then she found her voice her eyes bulged
she began to scream and scream
for a twofold agony began to attack her
on her head that golden circlet
became a filigree of flame melting and dripping
liquid fire and thon silky shawl
began to shrivel suck and paste itself
to her skin smothering her strangling
branding her soft flesh
as if she was fire itsel she leapt
rolling in agony trying to put herself out
no one but her father would have known her
blebbed and burning as she was
her melting flesh falling off her bones like
tallow from a flamboy or fat from a lamb on a spit
bubbling and bursting like
resin drops on a burning pine
till at last her horrid corpse
was blackened silent and still

we shrank back we were terrified
there was none of us would touch it
we'd seen we knew

till Kreon came poor man
ran in cried out fell on the corpse
cradling it sobbing
'Gods let me die with you!' he cried
'the parent should not outlive the child'
and he wept till his auld eyes could weep nae mair
and he was all gret oot
but when he went to staun up
here did the corpse no stick to him

as ivy clings to laurel   and it was
a dance macabre right enough
as the auld fellow tried to struggle free
and the deid weight of the deid daughter
pu'ed him to his knees again   the sair fecht of it
tearing his auld flesh from his aged bones
till at last he snuffed it   croaked
and there they lie
father on top of daughter   corpse on corpse
in a horrid parody of an unnatural embrace

the Gods are good
somebody was listening when he cried 'I want to die'
it could be said he   right royal   got his wish

and that's that
no surprise to you   Medea
by the Gods I'm feart frae you
mair feart even than I am feart o Jason
and the soldiers he'll bring with him
to torch this place

> *The* MANSERVANT *runs to the frozen-in-fear* NURSE *and
> shakes her.*

MANSERVANT

they'll kill us

I don't think we have snowball in hell's chance
but we maun
run auld yin   run

NURSE

I canna

> *The* MANSERVANT *– getting nowhere – flees in terror.*

CHORUS

Jason has suffered most horribly the day
as he well deserved to   truly
but that poor silly bairn   the bride
born to the bad fate of being Kreon's daughter
that same fate sent you Jason   death for a bride
and   for your honeymoon destination   hell

MEDEA

friends   nothing for it now
there is one way   and quickly
delay would be fatal   savage revenge comes running
another's hand   not a mother's loving hand
would kill my children

ring your heart in steel
raise your hand   that sword   do it!
flesh of my own flesh   this bitter place
where I must kill to prove my love

MEDEA *goes inside to do it.*

CHORUS

Gods stop her   if Gods you are!
Mother Earth open up and swallow her now
before she forever defiles you
with the spilt blood of her own children
the eye of the Sun that is too bright to look upon
look down   stop her in her tracks
burn her to a cinder
let the light reject her utterly   but stop her

pointless   the pain of giving birth to them?
useless   your love of them?
it was for them   to get your bairns
you braved those narrow straits
between those jagged bruise-coloured rocks
sailed close to death   and no for Jason

your raging heart!
remember the price the Gods exact
for the stain of spilt kin blood

Three deathknell sounds ring out.

you're stone   you're iron
your heart is nothing human
sex   makes birth   makes death
but here is a broken circle
here is nothing natural

JASON *enters.*

JASON

where is she?
that   monster is she in there?
or did she run   no hiding place
no hole in the earth   nowhere can she escape
the royal vengeance that hunts her down
I'm here to get my children   before some one
kills them for their mother's crime!

JASON *enters the house.*

CHORUS

Jason   you poor man
sorrow   you don't know
you don't yet know the half of it

> *That cry from* JASON. *A silence.* JASON *re-enters, a broken
> and emptied out man.* MEDEA *re-enters calm and cold.*

JASON

my children

MEDEA

you don't feel it yet   when you're old you will

JASON

my boys   my darling girl
you killed them

MEDEA

to kill you Jason   while you are still alive

JASON

you have put yourself beyond all pity
I wish you dead   but to touch you
even with my sword's tip would disgust me

MEDEA

nothing you do to me can touch me now
we're out of reach   beyond you

JASON

let me bury my children

MEDEA
they are not dead to me

JASON
out of their bright wounds their avenging furies swarm!
justice   blood for blood

MEDEA
flesh of my flesh   revenge

JASON
I must have been mad   was mad for you
I did not know you
I know you now!

MEDEA
tigress?   fury?   harpy?   witch?   she-wolf?
monster?   yes I am
for I have torn out your heart and devoured it

JASON
your pain is just as bad as mine

MEDEA
wrong   for I have your pain to comfort me

JASON
children   the mother you had

MEDEA
children   the father you had
end of story

JASON
it's over   it's all over

MEDEA
it will never be over   end of story

JASON
I wish I had never held you
a beautiful monster in my arms
I wish I had never turned to you in the night
never felt my seed spurt to your foul womb
never let you give birth
to this

The NURSE *starts muttering a version of her lines from the
very beginning of the play.*

NURSE

I wish to all the Gods it had never sailed   the Argo
had never set its proud prow atween the humped blue rocks
forced itsel through straits
to land on unlucky Kolchis

At this point JASON *begins to repeat his last speech as the*
NURSE *continues hers. The beginning of a building
cacophony.*

JASON

/ I wish I had never held you
I wish I had never turned to you in the night
never felt my seed spurt to your foul womb
never let you give birth
to this

NURSE

/ why did the sun ever heat up the soil
in which there split that seed
that sproutit from sapling to a tall tree of girth enough
to be felled to build its keel?

*Cacophony which builds and increases as the chorus too join
in at this point with both the* NURSE *continuing, and
simultaneously* JASON *repeating once more this version of
his final speech.*

CHORUS

/ the Gods look down
expect the unexpected
what we wish for   work for   plan for   hope for
think is bound to happen   won't

NURSE

/ why was it ever oared?
why crewed wi heroes fit to filch the Golden Fleece?
if no   my lady Medea
would never then have sailed wi Jason

Exactly on the NURSE*'s uttering of this, his name,
cacophony over.*

A final sound. Then in the clean silence, clearly and simply –

daft for him   doted!   fated   damned

CHORUS

the Gods look down
expect the unexpected
what we wish for   work for   plan for   hope for
think is bound to happen   won't
what is fated   will

end of story

End.